Old PORTISHEAD

by
John Macleay

Battery Point is a bracing spot with an outlook towards the Welsh coast and extensive views upstream and down-channel. As far as this group's concerned, though, they are the view. A feature of 'seaside tarriance' in the early 1900s was the formality of attire, a world away from today's sweatshirts, t-shirts and trainers.

First published in the United Kingdom, 2001,
by Stenlake Publishing,
Telephone / Fax: 01290 551122

ISBN 1 84033 162 3

FURTHER READING
Bryan Brown and John Loosely, *Book of Portishead*, Barracuda
    Books.
Eve Wigan, *A Tale of Gordano*, Wessex Press.
Eve Wigan, *Portishead Parish History*, Barnicoatt and Pearce.
Portishead & North Weston – Millennium Town Guide, Burrows
    Communications Ltd.

ACKNOWLEDGEMENTS
My thanks to local author Ken Crowhurst of the Portishead
Gordano Society and to the helpful staff at Bristol's College
Green Library and Portishead Public Library. Thanks also to
Tony Hardesty of the Approach Golf Course, Portishead, and
to Dave and Wendy who saw a little car ride as the quickest
answer to some of my queries.

Now simply Valley Road on the map, Nightingale Valley Road
was once a mere lane swallowed up in woodland. The road is
today wider but no less steep. Inevitably, there's increased
traffic but it's still a lovely area. Much of it is nature reserve,
taking in ancient woods and worked-out quarries favourable
to birds of prey.

INTRODUCTION

ST. PETER'S CHURCH PORTISHEAD. F.W.A.

Portishead has had various changes of name down the centuries, having been known as Portsheved, Porstsheve, Portishyde, Portherie, or, still in use, Posset. Whether the name denotes 'port by the ridge' or 'port by the headland', the area with its commanding outlook and the shelter of the Pill (derived from the old Welsh word indicating a tidal creek) inevitably invited settlement and, as evidence of encampments and smelters show, this had occurred by 2000 BC. The Romans may have erected a fort on the strategically important Point and other remains from their occupation have been found. After the establishment of Christianity, the area's history is hazy and largely quiet, but in the aftermath of the Norman Conquest many of the local families had been ousted by French families. The Domesday Book of 1086 shows that the vicinity's main asset was a mill, powered by the Wellhay stream, but by that time the quiet anchorage afforded by the Pill probably saw its regular use as a base for short trading voyages.

Through the centuries merchants and corporations in Bristol had purchased land and property in and around Portishead, many acquiring the equivalent of a 'weekend residence' within a ten mile ride or sail from the city. The local 'fyrd' (militia) was mobilised against the Armada in 1588 and the Elizabethan age saw Bristol prosper as trading links were developed with America and the Indies. For all that it was navigationally a 'dead-end', the Pill took its own small part in this trade, as well as possibly being part of the local black economy of the day, created by smuggling. During these centuries, agricultural progress was also made, particularly by the Gordon family, Scots who had made fortunes in the Caribbean. They were eventual purchasers of the mill and drained much marshy ground for farming.

By the end of the eighteenth century, the wealthy had become aware of the potential of the pleasing coastline and resorts came into being. By the 1850s Clevedon, which was served by a railway, had become the most popular of these. Portishead, already with a pier and hotel, both built in the 1830s, then got its own rail link with Bristol and subsequently it became known to the less well-off holidaymakers who were swift to appreciate its attractions. The present pier was constructed in 1869, beckoning new industries, and the holiday trade along with industrial development became the basis for the local economy well into the twentieth century.

Even now, the 'God's Acre' around St Peter's Church seems to nurse memories of pre-reformation times. Close by can be found a twelfth century manor (although its hexagonal tower is an Elizabethan addition), while the church features a minstrel's gallery, a Norman font, a mass dial and a Sanctus bell from mediaeval times. Here too can be found the restored, re-sited village cross which may date from Saxon times. It was moved to this location due to Portishead's expansion in the late eighteenth century.

PORTISHEAD PIER.

While arguably more functional than scenic, Portishead Pier provided a popular stroll as the writer of the message on this postcard verified. Built in 1869, it is still a terrific vantage point for watching shipping. At anchor is the TS *Formidable* which was originally brought here in 1869 and finally towed away in 1906, the latest date at which this photo could have been taken.

A boat drill in progress on TS *Formidable*. The ship was 240 feet long and weighed 2,250 tons. Her deck was some fifty feet above the water and she once carried a complement of eighty cannon. She was 'a training ship for homeless and destitute boys of the port of Bristol' and it was hoped this purpose would furnish 'potential good seaman material'. 'Prevention Better Than Cure' proclaimed the ship's motto, a bread and water diet or solitary confinement being available as either cure or preventive measure. And if she wasn't ruled with the proverbial rod of iron, there was liberal use of the birch rod. Despite the apparent harshness, many ex-trainees spoke fondly of their time on board 'the old tub'.

NATIONAL NAUTICAL SCHOOL, PORTISHEAD. (37.)   E. H. WRIGHT.

In the first years of the twentieth century, fifteen acres overlooking Black Nore Point were chosen to accommodate this striking building, a shore-based replacement for the *Formidable* which was barely seaworthy by then. It retained the ship's mizzen mast (pictured on the far right) and the rigorous training schedule didn't leave a lot of time for mutinous brooding; boat handling, navigation, band music, gunnery, musketry, fencing, carpentry, tailoring and even haircutting (probably with a limited choice of styles) were all taught here. Closed in 1982, the school has now been converted into a residential complex. The flag staff has been re-sited and the arches cover a parking area.

Lighthouse and National Nautical School, Portishead.

70844. J.V.

The Nautical School has sometimes been referred to as the 'reform school', implying that at certain times not every entrant here was a volunteer. However, in actual fact the school prepared trainees for service in both the merchant marine and the Royal Navy (or 'Grey Funnel Line' as it was facetiously called by merchant seamen). Visible here is the slipway on which launching procedures were practised, but the curriculum was further extended to include instruction in building, decorating, electrics, catering and classroom subjects. There are indications that the regime was severe but at least the accommodation was an improvement on an ageing, wooden-hulled, one-time ship of the line.

7

When the Romans started using the Pill as an occupational port from AD 43, it was already in use as a trading base with nearby Wales. When purchased by Bristol in the late 1700s, public rights were retained to the established wharf. Further development might have followed in the 1830s when the Great Western Railway sought to establish a regular transatlantic run with its steamship, the *Great Western*. Due to the Pill's proximity to the Bristol Channel, the company's engineer, Isambard Kingdom Brunel, favoured it as the ship's terminal, but by using the established Bristol docks the company was able to avoid the outlay for excavation and development. Brunel, however, continued to update his plans with endless memoranda which he carried literally 'under his hat', a habit of his. The *Great Western* did the Bristol–New York run from 1838.

Soon after the construction of the pier and dock in the 1860s, wharves, mills, factories, brickworks and a granary sprung up around the mouth of the Pill. Later these were joined by chemical plants and two power stations, the first of which opened in 1929 and the other in 1959, at which time a phosphorus plant was also established. All of this unsightly commercial development was fortunately hidden from the tourists by Woodhill, although the Pill still made an ideal sheltered halt for craft coming down-river from Bristol, boosting Portishead's appeal as a convenient 'happy marine retreat'.

Although this postcard was sent in October 1945, the picture itself would have dated from before 1939 as the docks were a restricted area throughout the war. It was during the war that the docks saw its busiest period as it played a vital role in both unloading supplies and shipping them out to the Normandy beachheads. After 1945 a gradual decline in shipping began. However, as an industrial zone it was to see further expansion, a second generating station being commissioned in the late 1950s. It ceased to function as a port in 1992 and all of the industrial landmarks have been cleared away for Portishead Quays which is still under construction and will combine, leisure, shopping, commercial and residential areas.

"WESTWARD BOUND"
ROYAL GEORGE OFF PORTISHEAD.

The deep water shipping channel which clips the shoreline here must have delighted generations of visitors, alarmed many ships' masters and allowed many emigrants a final poignant view of the homeland. Not the *Royal George* of Cowper's poem 'Toll for the dead . . .', this large mail vessel did a fortnightly run out of Avonmouth, often with a complement of Canada-bound emigrants. Requisitioned at the start of the First World War, she was sold to Cunard in 1919 (the year in which this card was mailed) but went to the breaker's yard three years later. Hereabouts is the second greatest tidal rise and fall in the world (forty-five feet). Only Nova Scotia's Bay of Fundy has a greater tidal range.

P.S. "ALBION" ASHORE

If anything, this picture of PS *Albion* 'ashore' showed the need for the lighthouse on Black Nore Point, and if Captain Webber, master of this paddle steamer, had a sense of humour he may have seen the joke in running his vessel aground on 1 April, 1907. Happily, with the aid of seven tugs, this Clydebank-built ship was refloated on the evening tide. She saw a further fourteen years service. A century and a half earlier such an event might have been seen as another 'occasional profit' by the locals. Their alleged predilection for plunder was viewed as 'grievous' by Bristol merchants, presumably as it grievously infringed upon their monopoly.

P.C. 40725 Portishead Lighthouse.

The Mariners' Path, possibly part of the ancient Wansdyke which was a forty mile earthwork running from Portishead to Wiltshire, wasn't exclusively trodden by seafarers as, at one time, there were enough hands ashore eager to convey illicit cargoes of smuggled brandy along the route to discreet 'drops' close by. The path goes past the nautical school (now called Fedden Village) and the lighthouse still stands. The precariously tilted structure on the right may have been the tearoom known as the Beehive. Needless to say, it is no longer standing.

The Rocks, Portishead

Commanding the approaches to both the Avon and Severn, the Rocks was a logical spot to fortify and man a lookout. The area was fiercely, if briefly, defended by Royalists in the Civil War, its eventual capture leading to Prince Rupert's surrender of Bristol. A small, squat, functional lighthouse stands here now and a recent suggestion that it might be removed looked as though it might spark off as spirited a resistance.

14

View of Rocks below Golf House.
Portishead

This postcard shows a pleasant stretch of shoreline beneath the Mariners' Path, quite near to the golf course. It's not hugely changed today, but this sort of rock is subject to constant erosion so that access to this favourite bathing spot is now less easy than it once was. In the background are the Rocks.

A refreshing attempt to get away from robins and holly on the part of local postcard publisher E.H. Wright, but the image of naked feet immersed in a chilly rock pool doesn't seem all that conducive to bonhommie and yuletide cheer. Still, as such cards were produced well in advance, we can be reasonably certain that these young ladies weren't hauled away from their Christmas dinners to pose for this shot.

Beach Villas & Esplanade, Portishead

Like several postcards in this collection, this was sent to a Bristol address, probably by a holidaying neighbour. This indicates the affection the city folk held for Portishead, even if one did complain, 'hills everywhere; you've even got to go uphill to get to the beach.' This is true as the shore is separated from the village by a long ridge.

Esplanade & Battery Point. Portishead. 604

A view of the Severn's Welsh shore, but Denny Island is all but obscured by the lady's outsize headgear. The two mile distant, hump-backed islet is a handy perch for all those birds partial to the crawling contents of estuarine mud. Battery Point, which was fortified or garrisoned at different periods, is clear of development and probably this dates the picture to the inter-war years.

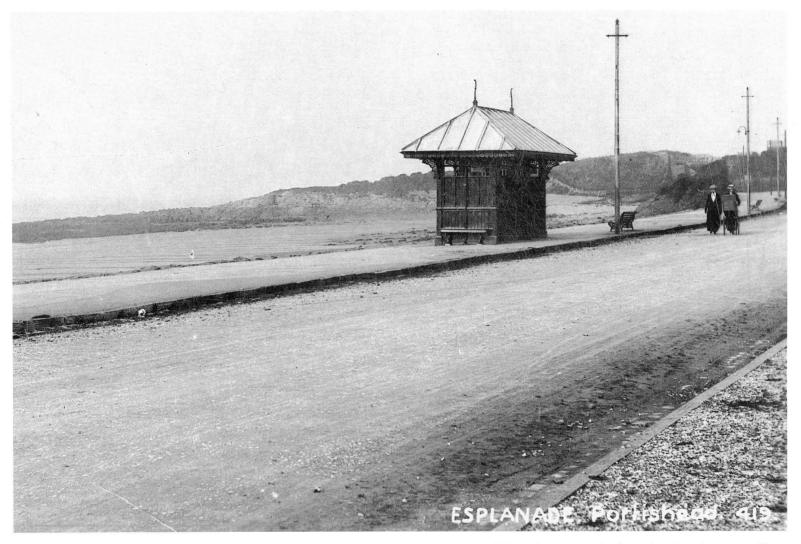

ESPLANADE Portishead 419

After the First World War, enterprising use was made of the battery buildings as tearooms and the no-longer-restricted area functioned as a sort of low-key pleasure garden. Among the delights one could find there were 'refined displays of conjuring and ventriloqual entertainments'.

Esplanade & Putting Green. Portishead.

Westfield. 503

A view of the esplanade, looking towards the golf links, probably from the 1930s. The putting green is no longer in existence but there is a nearby 'pitch and putt' course as well as facilities for tennis and cricket. These are merely superficial changes, the esplanade being little altered today.

On the seaward side of the lake is the beach shelter that's such a prominent feature on the previous card. When this picture was taken there appear to have been no buildings on the far side of the lake, but today the curving road swings up past the new swimming pool.

PORTISHEAD BATTERY POINT, FROM NORE ROAD   53103

A view from about the same position as the previous picture, but taken a little later. It shows the strategic importance of the Point which was garrisoned during Tudor times, the Civil War, and later, during the years of threatened Napoleonic invasion. During the Second World War it was once again out of bounds. Denny Island is in the distance, on the left of the picture.

In the Edwardian era being at leisure was no excuse for allowing standards of dress to lapse and the moustachioed man in the centre of the picture was probably the sort who would look, as well as feel, naked without his brolly. 'All is bowery and cool and still' commented one of the district's admirers. Bowery yes, but seemingly too cool for most of this party to risk removing their outer garments. This walk through ancient woodland in the Eastwood/Woodhill area is still pleasant today, if no longer so romantically lit. This being the only lamp in view, it was probably the last (or first) on the lamplighter's beat.

The steepness of the small but challenging Approach Golf Course must have resulted in an awful lot of lost golf balls and the stony beach beyond the Mariners' Path couldn't have made finding them easy. As there is no evidence of the small lighthouse on Battery Point (erected in the 1930s), this picture was probably taken in the twenties. The course was designed in 1908 by Harry Vardon and replaced that of the earlier Portishead Golf Club, although it was ploughed up in both world wars (even when such land wasn't put to agricultural use, it was reasoned that the plough furrows on sloping ground would at least slow down enemy troops in the event of a landing). The course now has neither club nor clubhouse, the nearby Windmill Inn being a restaurant, and is run by the North Somerset local authority.

MARINE LAKE. Portishead.

The Marine Lake was an early twentieth century job-creation project, excavated and constructed by the unemployed of Portishead and Bristol in 1910. Happily, in these times of high maintenance costs, liability and litigation, boats can still be hired here.

PORTISHEAD MARINE LAKE

The low bridge at the Marine Lake must have put this stretch out of bounds of rowing craft, possibly to allow youngsters to sail their model boats, such as the one displayed by the lad on the left. This still goes on even on winter Sundays, although the boats are now high-tech, high speed, remote controlled affairs. Despite the austere, formal layout, the lake has become a good spot for some undemanding bird-watching as winter storms drive wildfowl and waders ashore to rest here.

Marine Lake, Portishead

The Rodmoor, dug out to create the lake, had been scrubby marsh land, long used as something of a local dump, as workers discovered when they unearthed 3,000 year-old polished axe-heads.

Parkhurst is a decidedly incongruous name for what is likely to have been a guest-house when we recall a better-known establishment with the same name on the Isle Of Wight. There the policy certainly was never 'feel free to come and go as you please'. This card was mailed on 7 August 1914, only days before the start of the First World War. During both world wars postcard production not only dropped off, but commercial photography was discouraged in 'sensitive' areas. Even seemingly innocuous views, like those included in this book, could be used by the enemy to build up a picture of a projected target zone or invasion area.

BEACH COTTAGE TEA GARDEN, PORTISHEAD. E.H.W.

This postcard is reminiscent of something painted by Arthur Rackham, tempting us to look among the greenery for a witch awaiting an opportunity to join her two 'familiars'. The sender of the card records how, in delightful weather, 'we had refreshment yesterday' at this spot. Was that on recommendation of the cats who have all the assurance of regular customers? A picture pleasing to the romantically inclined, but likely to induce heart-attacks in environmental health officers.

Whatever tenuous connection the Waverley Guest House had with Sir Walter Scott's novels, it's no contender for any architectural awards. However, the wires indicate a telephone connection and it also had its own stationery (well, this postcard anyway). No doubt it was a welcoming home-from-home for generations of Bristolians.

OLD COTTAGE PORTISHEAD. E.H.W.

Thatch is still fairly common in Somerset towns and villages, as are the heavy pantiles like those roofing the adjoining building. In the earlier part of the twentieth century though – all matter of maintenance and insurance costs aside – thatch fell into disfavour, some dwellings in Portishead being condemned as fire-hazards.

This view from the rising ground behind St Peters shows just why the Pill suggested itself to Brunel as an ideal terminal for his ship. It shows also why Woodhill had also been known as Salty Hill. Since *Formidable* is still at anchor this must be pre-1906, but already the industrialisation of the harbour area had begun. Always in the shadow of the vast Avonmouth Docks, Portishead was something of a localised concern. While it is closer to the seaboard, the Pill was limited by its small size, whereas the Avon is navigable all the way up to Bristol. However, local stone had been shipped across to Wales from Roman times, and from there the docks took in shipments of coal (although there had been some local mining) and timber. Among the later development was the famous Portishead Nail Company which ceased production there in the 1980s.

Portishead shewing Parish Church. 603.

One chronicler of the town in the early nineteenth century was gratified to see 'churches and places of worship well filled and solemnly attended', and even today there's a wide choice. With rectors dating back to the fourteenth century, St Peter's Church on the right is unquestionably the most handsome as well as the oldest of the local churches. The row of houses beyond St Peter's form part of High Street, while the open land in front of it has now been swallowed up by housing development.

July 1949 is the date of postage on this card and the Belisha beacon (so named after the minister who introduced them) started to become a common feature of British streets in the late forties. These predated zebra and pedestrian crossings. While the volume of traffic would hardly seem to justify its presence, signs on the left indicate a garage and by this time High Street had undergone much commercial development since its name was changed from Mill Street in the late eighteenth century (by that time the local water mill had declined in importance while the village had grown large enough to merit a 'High Street'). The trees on the right hand pavement have gone, but new trees have been planted in recent times.

High Street, Portishead

This is the view just a few yards along from the previous picture, although it dates from an earlier period. Quite how much earlier is difficult to determine. The trees are in good health, whereas in the previous picture they have been 'crowned' and the telegraph pole on the right bears a street sign. The only transport is literally one-horse-power, hence the unconcern with which someone is trundling a pram or pushcart along the middle of the street. The tower of St Peter's dominates the background of both pictures.

The foliage of Woodhill softens the long sloping line of roofs which follows the incline of Beach Road. This agreeable composition shows the substantial housing that the well-heeled of Bristol could afford and while Portishead as a resort may have lost out to its larger neighbours, Weston-super-Mare and Clevedon, it managed to avoid the brashness and vulgarities so often associated with bigger holiday centres.

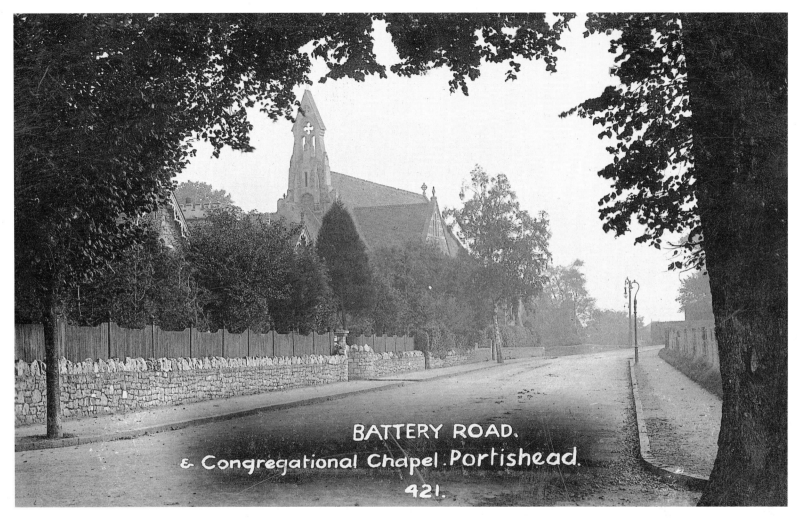

BATTERY ROAD.
& Congregational Chapel. Portishead.
421.

Dated 27 April 1915, the writer of this postcard professed an ignorance of the locality, not even having been 'up to the lakes very often', apparently because 'I don't travel far from home'. Home would seem to have been the nautical school as he further explains, 'they are allowing about 150 away . . . my name is in. We are to be inspected tomorrow by some general . . . it's been nothing but scrub out these last few days'. One hopes that after that, he enjoyed his leave.

ADELAIDE TERRACE.
FROM BEACH ROAD, PORTISHEAD.

36691.

The elegant Adelaide Terrace was named after William IV's wife and while its skyline is fussy by modern standards, it recalls an undeniably gracious era.

Adelaide Terrace, at the town end of Woodhill Road, was constructed in the 1830s. After Caroline Boyle, an early resident of this prestigious address, quarrelled with a local clergyman, she took to preaching herself and prefaced each of her sermons with 'I am the Right Honourable Catherine Boyle, lady-in-waiting to Her Majesty' (meaning Queen Adelaide, which was indeed true).

P.G. 40724 Portishead, Nore Road.

Nore Road, part of a busy route to Clevedon and Weston-super-Mare, is of necessity wider today, but the view across the golf course is unchanged. The clubhouse is now the Windmill Inn and while the wooden sails have gone, the stone-built mill is itself still tucked behind the building. Although not all golf pros or greenkeepers approved of the effect they have on the grass, it was customary to graze sheep on such courses.

Although no building remains, the spot where this farm stood on Nore Road is still discernible among all the later development. Possibly it was one of the farms built in the Gordano area in the 1820s by James Gordon, owner of West Indian plantations and once of the village water mill, but as it was no great distance from the Mariner's Path it may also have been used as a hiding place and distribution point for smuggled goods.

The message on the reverse of this card shows this house to be Severn Bank on Nore Road where possibly it stands today having undergone a name-change and a face-lift or two.

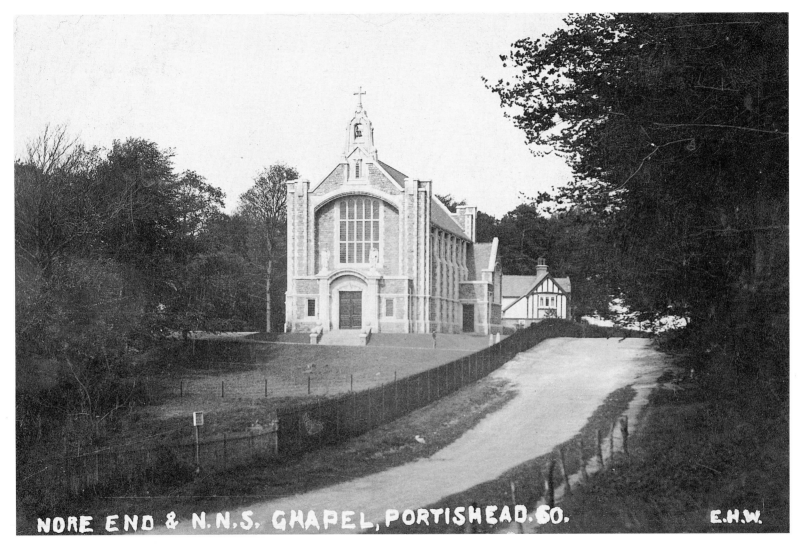

NORE END & N.N.S. CHAPEL, PORTISHEAD. 60.

E.H.W.

The Nautical School chapel still stands by the gates to Fedden Village. It houses a pulpit constructed from some timbers from the old *Formidable*. Holidaymakers liked to round off a Sunday with an evening service here.

With the beach hidden from view, and silos, chimneys and other structures that signposted the dock now cleared away, it's difficult from 'the village', as High Street is still known, to remember that Portishead is a coastal and riverside town. The vacant ground on the bottom right is now the site of the Portishead Quays development, but was in the past part of the 'meadow, pasture and scrubland' which belonged to the mill. The large white building beyond the curve in the rail tracks is now the White Lion pub and it stands on the site of the water mill which ground corn for the neighbourhood. The mill was mentioned in the Domesday Book and one of its stones is built into a wall nearby. With perseverance, evidence of the old railway, which closed in 1964, can still be located.

When the tourists had tired of sea-views, sunsets and salty air, they could always do a bit of trainspotting on the 'comic light railway', as the Weston, Clevedon & Portishead Light Railway was known. This is engine No.1, 'Clevedon', built in 1879 by Dubs, a German firm with workshops in Glasgow. The light railway started in 1897, although Portishead was not connected to it until 1907. It closed entirely in 1940.

A 64 h.p. Drewry railcar, No.5, built for the Southern Railway in 1928. It had seating capacity for twenty-two and was equipped with a separate luggage compartment. Purchased by the light railway in 1934, it was used for six years before being scrapped.

The engine 'Hesperus' was built in 1911 and saw service on the light railway until 1937. Its number was actually 1384, the final digit being here obscured by the head of the conductor, Mr Cullen.

This group of railway personnel are not named although in the pre-car era, when kids dutifully waved to train-drivers and families holidayed annually at the same resort, train and station staff were as much part of the holiday as beaches, boating lakes or woodland walks.

Occasionally the light railway bought its engines new, like this one built by Manning Wordle in 1919. A memo jotted on the back of the photograph urges the reader to 'note the solid wheels'. The coaches had previously seen service (perhaps on another line) as private saloons. This photo was in fact taken at Weston-super-Mare.